Well
Less

Feasts
Budget

Eat Well
For Less
Family Feasts on a Budget

Contents

Foreword

We love being part of *Eat Well for Less* because with every family we meet we face a new set of challenges to resolve, and we never quite know how it's all going to unfold! Saving money is brilliant, but what we really love is seeing a family cook and eat together. There's something magical about everyone sitting around a table, and it puts a smile on all their faces. So, what are you waiting for…?!

We've looked back through the series and pulled together a great selection of quick and easy recipes, all of which deliver tasty and nutritious meals that won't break the bank. It's time to eat well for less!

So many families we meet have fallen out of love with cooking, either because they can't find a meal that everyone will eat or because they feel there simply isn't enough time to cook from scratch. We hope this book will bring family mealtimes to life again and show that cooking can be fun, especially if you work together.

Some of the recipes here will show you how you can take a main dish and tweak it for those family members who are a bit 'fussy' because, believe us, you're not alone! Nearly everyone has a 'fussy eater' in their family and it's our job to help you get everyone sitting down together. Cooking different meals for different family members needs to stop!

As we always say, a little planning goes a long way, especially when it comes to getting the family eating together, but it does mean you need to plan together, too. Use this book as the inspiration to sit down as a group and work out what recipes you might be able to tweak to make everybody happy.

Another area that really works with family eating is getting some batch cooking done. If you find you have some spare time, over the weekend perhaps, have a look at some of our recipes that freeze well and save yourself some valuable time in the long run. Serve that chilli with rice today, then leftovers can be a tasty baked potato topping another day when you're short of time. Remember, cook once, eat twice… or three times, or even four…!

One last word from us… when you're doing your supermarket shop, just imagine we're watching you make all your purchases – what would we be saying?! And once you're home, why not try playing along and swap out some of your usual top branded products for better value alternatives? Just pop them into plain containers and see if the family notice – you might be pleasantly surprised at just how much you can get away with!

Gregg Wallace and Chris Bavin

Getting kitchen confident

We all know that cooking from scratch is cheaper than buying ready prepared food, but putting this into practice when you're new to cooking can feel a little daunting. Fear not though, it's not difficult if you keep it simple to start with and build your confidence before you move on to trickier dishes. Remember, at this stage what you dish up doesn't have to look perfect. As long as it tastes ok and is edible, it's a success, not a disaster!

First up, what are you going to cook? Start with simple, tried-and-tested recipes from trusted websites – and this book! – and, more importantly, pick something that looks appealing and that you think you will all want to eat. Don't attempt recipes that use unusual ingredients until you have developed your skills and feel confident to step outside your comfort zone. It's also a good idea to choose recipes that use only a few ingredients, as long lists of ingredients can be off-putting and send you straight to the ready-made jars and sauces in a panic.

Before you hit the shops, check your cupboards/fridge/freezer, then make a list of what you need and the relevant quantities of each ingredient. Remember all the planning advice – think about what you're cooking and when, and don't attempt to cook something new or tricky when you're short of time, otherwise you may get flustered.

Tip

Don't waste money on pre-prepared vegetables or fruit; peeling and chopping take just a few minutes and whole ingredients are much cheaper. Pre-chopped ingredients also deteriorate more quickly in your fridge; their cut surfaces are exposed to the air and will dry out, losing flavour and texture.

Get everything ready

Right, so are you armed with ingredients and a trusty recipe? You're almost ready to get started, just have a quick look at this list first...

- Organise your kitchen cupboards so you know where everything is, and try to keep them this way as it will make your cooking in a hurry really easy.
- Clear the work surface of any unnecessary clutter and give it a good wipe clean.

- Sharpen your kitchen knives, and check them regularly. Blunt tools make food preparation much harder, plus they are potentially more dangerous to use.
- Remove any butter, eggs, etc., from the fridge to soften or warm up to room temperature if the recipe recommends it.
- If the recipe tells you to preheat the oven at the beginning, turn it on now. Grease and line any tins at the start, too.

- If you're using frozen ingredients, check with the recipe if they should be defrosted first. If so, you might need to build in time for this, or carefully defrost them in a microwave oven, if you have one. This is particularly important for meat, chicken or fish, however, vegetables will defrost quickly during cooking.
- Read the recipe properly and get out all the ingredients and equipment you are going to need, to save you digging around in the fridge or cupboards halfway through cooking. If you are missing an ingredient, see if it's something you can easily substitute with something you do have.

- If your kitchen bin isn't right by your work surface, keep a large bowl to one side to chuck in waste wrappers and peelings, etc., as you cook. This makes it much easier to clear up at the end.

Get cooking

So, it's time to get cooking. Wash your hands and tie back long hair, then put on a clean apron to protect your clothes – this could get messy!

First tip is to follow the recipe carefully. This is most important if you are baking – the ingredient quantities listed are important here and it's not recommended to swap things in or out until you really know how to bake – it could mean the difference between a towering fluffy sponge layer cake and a sad-looking pile of flat biscuit-like sponges. You have been warned!

However, tweaking non-baking recipes is usually quite straightforward and you can pretty safely ring the changes. If you find you've forgotten an ingredient, don't panic, swap it out for something you do have. For example, if your kids don't like French beans, use broccoli instead. With practice and a lot of tasting you'll find these decisions really easy and you won't worry about going off-recipe!

When you're cooking rice, pasta, pulses, etc., check the instructions on the packaging. Some types of rice should be rinsed before cooking to remove the starch that makes grains stick together when cooked; if so, tip the rice into a sieve and set it under cold running water. Some dried beans may need soaking before use – sometimes overnight – so check the packet and build in time. Tinned beans are good to go! Check the cooking times on all packets, too, as these vary depending on type and brand. If in doubt, test the ingredient just before the end of the cooking time by scooping a little out.

Tip

Keep a record of all the recipes that worked well or were popular with the family. Having a good stash of staple recipes will make life easier and give you kitchen confidence.

Portion sizes

Healthy eating is all about eating well, but not overeating. If you're new to cooking, it can be tricky to know what constitutes a portion, particularly if you aren't following a recipe to the letter or are adding sides and extras. To make this easier, a few of the more popular ingredients are listed here to give you an idea of how much to use per person, per day. These are the recommended measurements for people maintaining their current weight, but bear in mind if you want to lose weight you will need to eat fewer or smaller portions.

Don't forget, weighing out food is an economical way of cooking as it reduces food waste – so those extra couple of minutes measuring can save you money!

- ✔ 30g breakfast cereal
- ✔ 5 × 80g servings of different fruit or veg (each about the size of your fist)
- ✔ 2 slices of bread
- ✔ 2 eggs
- ✔ 3 tsp butter, oil or other fat (max)
- ✔ 200ml milk
- ✔ 125g yoghurt
- ✔ 30g cheese (the size of two thumbs)
- ✔ 100g meat (the size of the palm of your hand and thickness of a deck of cards)
- ✔ 150g white fish (the size of your full hand)
- ✔ 100g oily fish
- ✔ 80g uncooked dried pasta/rice/ noodles (the size of your fist)
- ✔ 180g potato (the size of your fist)
- ✔ 80g small fruits (as much as can fit in your cupped hands)
- ✔ 20g chocolate (about 3–4 squares)

Healthy hygienic cooking

One of the great things about cooking from scratch is that you know exactly how the food has been prepared. Bearing that in mind, it's really important to follow good kitchen hygiene at all times to reduce any risk of transferring bacteria from raw foods to other ingredients.

Before you start cooking, clean work surfaces with a disinfectant spray and repeat whenever surfaces make contact with raw meats. Use kitchen paper for this and discard it immediately – don't use kitchen cloths, as you will just transfer the bacteria to somewhere else in the kitchen.

Keep separate chopping boards for preparing raw and cooked meat, poultry, fish and fruit and vegetables – getting them in different colours is a really helpful way of identifying them. Keep utensils separate, too, to avoid cross-contamination, and always wash your hands in between touching raw, cooked or ready-to-eat foods.

When preparing chicken, don't wash it first; any water splashing off the bird contains bacteria, which may splatter around the kitchen.

Of course, an important part of preparing food for your family or friends is making sure the meal is properly cooked! This is easily done once you know a few tricks of the trade. It is particularly important to check that meat, poultry and fish are properly cooked through.

Kitchen hygiene aside, to get the best texture and flavour you don't want to undercook or overcook, so here are a few tips to get it perfect every time.

Meat

(approximate timings for grilling meat)

Sirloin or rump steak – 1½–2 minutes on each side for rare; 3 minutes on each side for medium; about 4 minutes on each side for well done.

Fillet steak – 4 minutes on each side for rare; 5 minutes on each side for medium; about 6 minutes on each side for well done.

If in doubt, prod the cooked steak with your fingers – when rare it will feel soft, medium-rare will be a little bouncy and well done should be much firmer.

Pork chops – 10 minutes on each side; pork steaks slightly less.

Lamb chops – 10 minutes on each side; cutlets about 5 minutes on each side.

Tip

Give it a rest – set aside meat at room temperature for at least 5 minutes after cooking. It will stay hot for anything up to 10 minutes covered with foil. Giving it a rest allows the fibres of the meat to absorb its juices, making it wonderfully moist and tender.

Chicken

When cooking a whole bird, pierce the thickest part – the thigh – with a sharp knife. Once cooked, any juices coming out should be clear and the tip of the knife should be very hot. If not, return to the oven for another 5 minutes, then check again. For chicken breasts or drumsticks, cut into the thickest part of the meat and see if it is pink; if it is, it needs cooking for longer.

Fish

Test the thickest part of the fillet 2 minutes before the end of the suggested cooking time by carefully poking through it with the point of a sharp knife. Uncooked fish has a translucent colour and spongy texture, but when cooked it should be opaque and firm, flaking easily.

Seafood

Cooked prawns should be pink all the way through. Before cooking mussels, sharply tap any that are open on the worktop to see if they close shut. Discard any that remain open or are damaged. Once cooked, discard any mussels that are still shut as they are not safe to eat.

Stock up your store cupboard

If you're short of time or money, a well-stocked kitchen can be a godsend. A simple supper can be transformed with just a few dried herbs and spices, or stretched to feed extra mouths with the addition of a tin of beans or lentils, or it means you can just throw something together quicker than a pizza delivery!

It only takes a little planning to ensure that you have a fantastic back-up for a busy night or a treasure trove of goodies to perk up a few core ingredients. But before you fill your trolley, have a good clear out of your kitchen. See what you've got and check the use-by dates on the packets – if it's out of date, bin it. It's ok to be ruthless now, because you are about to change your bad habits for good…

Keeping a good selection of core ingredients to hand is also about storing them properly – otherwise you can find yourself wasting money by throwing things out that have gone off, or the flavour has deteriorated.

Essentially, food can be stored in three areas of your kitchen: cupboards and shelves, the fridge or the freezer (see page 34).

Cupboards and shelves

These are for the foods that should be stored at room temperature to keep them at their best – try to avoid having them near a heat source, though, as they will store longer and better in a cool, dark place. Cupboards are neat and keep contents out of sight, but shelves are also perfectly good if that's what you have. However, if your shelves are in a sunny spot, put ingredients in containers to keep the contents cool and out of direct light.

Foods that are suitable for room-temperature storage are:

Unopened tins and jars such as pesto, honey, sauces and pickles – once opened, many of these will need to be stored in the fridge, so check the packaging!
Flours, pasta, rice, noodles and dried pulses – once opened, store packets in airtight containers.

Oils and vinegars
Nuts, seeds and dried fruits – store in airtight containers to keep their texture.
Herbs and spices – keep these in airtight tins or spice jars.
Fresh foods – garlic, onions and shallots, tomatoes, potatoes and winter squash can be kept in a cool, dry place for up to 2 weeks. Don't put them in the fridge or they will lose a lot of their flavour. Putting onions and potatoes in hessian bags will extend their life, preventing them from growing shoots.
Bananas, citrus fruits and melons – fine on the worktop or kitchen table, but should be moved to the fridge once cut or they will dry out. Bananas emit ethylene, a natural ripening gas, which causes any ingredients around them to ripen faster, so don't leave these in the fruit bowl, keep them separate.

Foods for the fridge

The fridge is the invaluable invention that has made daily trips to the shops a thing of the past; fresh foods stay fresh in these cold boxes and the low temperature also prevents the growth of dangerous bacteria.

Foods that need to be in your fridge are:

Dairy products – put these on the top shelves where the temperature is most constant. Wrap cheese separately in greaseproof paper or pop into a loose plastic bag. Ensure butter is properly wrapped in foil or clingfilm.

Eggs – can last longer in their box on a shelf inside the fridge than if they are stored at room temperature – up to 3 weeks after the date of laying. However, do check the use-by date on the box, too. (If you're not sure if your eggs are ok to eat, see page 32 for testing tips.)

Vegetables – store these in perforated plastic bags in the salad drawer.

Fruit – store away from vegetables, particularly those fruits that produce ethylene, a natural ripening gas (this includes apples, bananas, stone fruits, mangoes, passion fruit, pears and kiwi fruit), so the veg keep longer. Wash fruit before use, but not before storing, as excess water speeds up decomposition. Whole lemons are best stored in the fruit bowl, but once zested, wrap them in clingfilm and pop in the fridge.

Herbs – trim a little off the base of sprigs of basil, parsley, coriander and other leafy herbs and pop them into a glass of water, loosely covered with a plastic bag, then put them in the fridge on a shelf where they won't get knocked over. Stored this way they should stay fresh for at least a week. Wrap herbs like thyme and rosemary in sheets of damp kitchen paper and layer them in plastic bags.

Meat and poultry – keep these at the bottom of the fridge (the coldest section) tightly wrapped so their juices don't transfer to other foods.

Fish – dry fish completely with kitchen paper and wrap in greaseproof paper before storing in the bottom of the fridge. It should keep for up to 2 days, but sniff it before you cook it; if it smells really fishy, throw it out.

Keeping your fridge happy

✔ To keep your food fresh, you need to keep your fridge happy. A few easy checks will mean less food wastage and lower electricity bills.

✔ Whenever you restock the fridge, move older items towards the front of the shelves so you use them first.

✔ When putting leftovers into the fridge, cool them quickly first and store when cold; hot food warms up the food and air around it, which affects the temperature of the fridge and encourages bacteria to grow.

✔ Keep the fridge at a constant temperature of 5°C or lower – you can buy a fridge thermometer cheaply and pop it inside if your fridge doesn't display the temperature. Don't overfill the fridge – air has to circulate to keep the temperature constant, otherwise the fridge uses more electricity to keep the food cool.

✔ Wipe up spills at once and clean drawers and shelves regularly to ensure that the fridge stays hygienic.

It's all in the planning!

Those of you familiar with *Eat Well for Less* will know that healthy eating on a budget is all in the planning. But don't feel intimidated by this – a little forethought will go a long way.

Get organised

Don't go shopping without a plan. Drifting around a supermarket will cost you – this is when most people waste money, by picking up items they fancy the look of, or appear to be a bargain, without actually thinking about how and when they'll use them. The same rule applies to shopping when you're tired or hungry – you'll find things creep into your basket that you didn't intend to buy. Shopping with children can also be problematic – by all means get them to help, but ensure that you know what they are putting into the basket, and steer them away from aisles with tempting treats!

So, before you head out, you need to make a list. But before you get to that, there are a couple more steps to take.

Plan your menus

Cooking from scratch is not just healthier for your body but healthier for your bank balance, too. So don't reach for the ready meals, keep turning these pages and get to the recipes. It's time to get to know your kitchen.

Once you get cooking, you won't look back. Start simply (see page 94) and expand your repertoire as you build your confidence. Don't just think about the meals that you eat at home, what about packed lunches for the kids or for yourself? Did you know that a working couple can spend around £40 a week on coffees, breakfasts, lunches and snacks? That's potentially over £2000 a year you could save just by thinking ahead! Packing your own lunch and treats and investing in a travel mug to take your first hot drink of the day with you, or a freshly made fruit smoothie for breakfast, will all make a difference.

So when you're next sitting down in front of the TV, arm yourself with these recipes and have a think about what you want to cook across the week ahead. Look at your calendar, see who's at home each night and when, and plan what you could cook. If you know that a certain night will be busy, with all the family coming and going, perhaps cook something simple that can be reheated or dipped into (see page 18). Try to plan a meat-free night, too – it's a healthy way to eat and as meat is one of the most expensive food ingredients, it also makes for a cheaper night (see page 24).

If you have one day a week where you have more time, cook double the amount of one recipe, then you can freeze some of it, ready to be defrosted and heated on a night when you're too tired or too busy to cook (see page 28). The extra time spent doing this on a quiet day is so worth it when dinner is already made on a busy night. If planning a whole week ahead is too much for you at first, plan a few days at a time until you get used to the new way of shopping and cooking.

Be sensible when planning your meals – think about the ingredients you're using and don't plan to use expensive ones. Try to use cheaper cuts of meat or ingredients that are in season (see below). Plan for treats, too. Eating well on a budget doesn't mean stripping out all the foods you look forward to, it's about eating them in moderation. So if you think you might crave a treat later in the week while you're transitioning to your new healthy eating regime, allow for this. But don't buy them – bake them. That way you can keep control of your budget and what goes into them. You can make fruit muffins, oat cookies and flapjacks with dried fruit. If you don't trust yourself around treats, bake a cake and freeze it, sliced, so you just take one piece at a time and you're not tempted to eat the whole lot in one go!

Think about the recipes and whether you want to double them up for another day, or cook them as they are. You can also stretch meals by adding in extra vegetables, tinned pulses or lentils, which will make the dish go further, replacing more expensive meat. This is a great opportunity to use leftovers or ends of vegetables lurking in the bottom of the fridge.

Foods that cut the cost of shopping

Cheaper cuts

The most expensive cuts of beef are sirloin, fillet and rib-eye, but if you really want a steak, flat iron steak makes a delicious cheaper alternative. If you are slow-cooking or using the pressure cooker, try using brisket or shin of beef, which will produce melt-in-the mouth textures when cooked this way.

Breast fillets are the most expensive chicken pieces, especially if they're skinless. Thighs or legs are much cheaper and full of flavour – particularly when cooked on the bone. Both are great roasted, and thighs are ideal for slow-cooking in stews or curries.

Eat with the seasons

Basically this means eating locally produced foods at the right time of year, when they're naturally at their best and most plentiful. When eaten out of season, foods are more expensive because they will either have been grown in warmer climes and flown into the UK, incurring export costs, or grown under heat, which has its own energy expenses for the producer. Not only is eating seasonally cheaper to the consumer and better for the environment, the foods taste better, too.

Tip

Not sure what's in season? Go online and print out a seasonal calendar to remind you what's in season when and stick it on your fridge.

Fill your freezer

Frozen foods are often cheaper than fresh, and fresher, because they're frozen so quickly after picking; even locally produced fresh foods will have lost about half their original amount of nutrients by the time they reach the supermarket shelves. Keeping a stock of frozen ingredients also means you're less likely to waste them by forgetting about them in the fridge, and they're on hand to form the base of a speedy meal (see page 34).

Wonky, weird and wonderful

Embrace the less-than-perfect produce. If fruit and vegetables are just going to be chopped or mashed, they don't need to be beautiful. Many of these fruit and vegetables can be found in local markets or in special sections in some supermarkets. Buying them means the products that don't meet the specifications of some of the supermarkets don't get wasted, so not only are you helping your bank balance, you're also helping out the food producers and the nation to reduce their wastage.

Going shopping

Once you've planned your meals, write a shopping list. Check your cupboards, fridge and freezer to see which ingredients you've already got, then make a list of everything else you need. Most shopping lists include items that you've run out of or don't have, but do you actually need them?

Ideally, you want to make this shop the big one of the week and avoid any further trips – it's nipping out for milk or something else that costs, as you'll rarely leave the shop armed only with the thing you came in for… If you do have to pop out, walk to the shops and take only one shopping bag, and when you're in there grab a basket – this will encourage you to buy less as you won't want to carry it all home.

In the supermarket, stick to the list. Don't get sidetracked by tempting offers or treats, no matter how good they look. If there are offers, look at them carefully. Is it really cheaper to buy three rather than two, or buy one and get one free; is £3 for two items individually priced at £1.50 each a bargain? Look at the weights of the packets and see if it really is a good deal. Of course, these deals can be great value, but only if you use everything before it goes off (see page 30), otherwise if it just hits the bin it's money literally thrown away.

Get online

Online shopping can be a lifesaver for busy families. It means you can get your groceries conveniently delivered to your door at a time that suits you, but it's also a brilliant way to stop yourself overspending. You have total control of what's going into your basket, and you're less likely to get distracted by in-store offers.

Work out your budget

For one week, keep track of how much you spend – that's the big shop and every little trip out to pick up milk, the lunches, coffees, snacks and all the other bits. It can be quite a revelation. Then think about how that adds up over a month, and a year. Is it affordable within your salary and budget? No? Then decide what is and aim to stick to that budget.

Take into consideration all your major expenditure, such as rent/mortgage and utility bills, then see what you have left. If you're not sure what sort of budget you should be thinking about, try to allocate 10–15 per cent of your net income to food and grocery shopping.

Unfortunately, the price of food has soared in recent years, and experts think these costs are not likely to lower in the near future, so this really is the time to get thrifty. When you next go shopping, have a good look at your receipt and see where your spending is greatest. Is there anything on there you really don't need? Have you paid a lot more for something you could have got cheaper elsewhere, or could you have bought a less expensive but pretty much comparable product (for example, the shop's or supermarket's own brand)?

One way of keeping to your budget is to take cash with you – no cards – and only what you have budgeted for. That way you simply can't overspend.

Top tips

✔ Work out if products are good value by comparing prices per 100g.

✔ Walk past promotions, think about them and then go back if you really think they're worth it and you'll use the products.

✔ If you buy offers, use them as soon as possible (especially fresh foods). If you don't think you'll get the chance to use the fresh food offers quickly, freeze them when you get home to use at a later date.

✔ Get yourself a stash of quick, easy recipes that you can cook in minutes so you resist the temptation of buying ready meals.

✘ Don't take the oldest stock with soonest use-by date, reach to the back of the shelf to get the items with the longest shelf-life.

✘ Don't buy pre-cut and pre-prepped fruit, veggies and salad, they can cost twice as much as the whole ingredients, lose their nutrients rapidly and deteriorate quicker than the unprepared product.

Cooking for the family

Cooking for the family can be an added stress, especially in busy households. For most families the ideal is to just prepare one meal that everyone can share, but the reality is that the pace of modern life doesn't always mean that's possible. Often members of the family arrive home at different times due to after-work or after-school activities, or perhaps the children are fussy eaters or don't like the same foods as the adults. Other families may include vegetarians or vegans, or those who have dietary restrictions because of allergies or intolerances. These sorts of considerations require good menu planning so that everyone gets fed without you spending the entire evening in the kitchen, or having to waste food unnecessarily. So to keep sane, on budget and have a happy, well-fed family, here are a few useful tips:

For the busy family

✔ Cook one-pot meals and either keep them warm in a low oven or in a slow cooker, so that dinner is piping hot and ready when latecomers walk through the door.

✔ Feed most of the family but reserve a plateful of food that can be reheated in the microwave or on the hob. You may need to think a bit more about what to cook, because some foods may not reheat well – for instance, be careful when reheating rice (see page 31 for tips on reheating rice), and anything crunchy will lose its texture and go soggy in the microwave. In general, soups, casseroles and foods in sauces are all good for reheating.

✔ Serve up something that tastes good hot or cold, such as a quiche or omelette, or baked potatoes that can be kept warm with easy fillings added from the fridge or store cupboard, such as grated cheese, baked beans, bacon or tinned tuna.

To keep everyone happy

✔ Choose recipes that most family members like, or at least have a good few ingredients in stock that they will eat. A couple of different vegetables or sides will mean that everyone eats something, but don't prepare more than that or you'll feel like you're cooking separate meals again!

✘ Don't make food too spicy, unless your kids' taste buds are adapted to it. If the adults like their food with a kick or well-seasoned, give the children their portions first before adding chilli sauce or seasoning, or split the food into two pots when cooking.

✔ Of course, the children's favourites can still be popular with the whole family. Try making your own healthy versions of chicken nuggets, pizzas, burgers and chips.

✔ If you have a vegetarian or vegan in the family, try one meat-free night a week (see page 24) to make life easier (not to mention healthier!) for all, or use recipes that can be adapted for vegetarians, perhaps dividing into two pans when cooking.

✔ For food allergies and intolerances, depending on the severity of them, you need to decide whether or not it is better to avoid using that ingredient entirely (see opposite).

Catering for special diets

It is now estimated that up to 50 per cent of children in this country have some form of food allergy or intolerance. Some allergies will lessen or disappear as children grow up, but some may be there for life. If you think a member of your family may have an allergy or intolerance, get medical advice before you make any major changes to their diet.

If the allergy is severe, it can be a good idea to remove the food causing the reaction from the diet of the whole family. If it's just an intolerance, you can still cook it for the rest of the family. This doesn't have to mean big changes, though; for instance, when serving pasta to a coeliac or gluten-intolerant, you could just serve up the same gluten-free sauce alongside a bowl of gluten-free pasta.

If you have a vegetarian or vegan in the family, you could just make some tweaks to family meals; it could be as simple as serving a vegetarian main alongside the same sides as the rest of the family, or perhaps cooking a whole dish without meat.

The Caans

Allergy or intolerance?

A food allergy occurs when the body's immune system reacts to a certain food type. The effects – generally a rash, wheezing or itching, but sometimes more severe reactions – are apparent within an hour or two, sometimes quicker, and may need some form of medication, or medical attention, if severe. The most common allergies are to fish, shellfish, wheat and nuts. Younger children may have allergies to milk and eggs.

A food intolerance, on the other hand, does not affect the immune system and may cause a less serious reaction – bloating or stomach cramps – perhaps over time rather than quickly. Those with an allergy to a certain foodstuff cannot eat that ingredient, whereas those with an intolerance may eat it, but only in small quantities and infrequently.

Fussy eating

Do mealtimes with your children feel like a battle? Don't worry, you are not alone! The good news is that most children do grow out of this, but it can be really frustrating and just loads up the pressure on you when you're cooking for the family. So, here are a few tips to restore calm to your kitchen when eating with little ones and get everyone on track to eating together.

Keep a routine for mealtimes
Have three meals a day and only offer limited amounts of healthy snacks in between.

Regularly introduce new foods
If you get a flat no, try serving them alongside something they're familiar with and like. Steer clear of offering unhealthy options, though. The more they see it, the more comfortable they will be with it – some children need to see a new food up to ten times before they accept it, so don't give up.

Think about the portion sizes
Use a child's-size plate and don't overload it; make sure you can see plenty of the plate. Start with a small portion if your child struggles, you can offer more later if they're still hungry. Don't put a child under pressure to finish everything.

Whet their appetite
If a very small child is too hungry to wait for supper, offer them a healthy snack they like that tastes sweet rather than savoury. Apple slices, grapes or melon will ease their hunger so they are in a better frame of mind to eat, with the added bonus of helping them towards their 5 a day.

Eat together
Your child will be more inclined to eat if they see you tucking into the same thing or eating with them. However, it doesn't have to be you they eat with, you could invite their friends over for tea instead.

Let little ones feed themeselves
You may be tempted to feed young children, but with a growing sense of independence, it is

Eating together

Sitting together around the kitchen table not only helps children to understand the work that goes into preparing food and appreciate food, but it's also a good opportunity for them to learn how to listen to others, take part in conversations, and observe good table manners. Above all, it's a really great way to get proper family time together and catch up on each other's days!

The Butlers

important to let them feed themselves. Some of the battle may be about wanting to do it, so let them. The mess is worth it if it means they develop a taste for new foods. Finger foods are great for this.

Offer incentives

Older children might be persuaded to eat different foods if they think there's something in it for them! Try a reward scheme like a sticker chart in the kitchen. Get the children to decorate it themselves to make it personal, then reward them with a sticker every time they try something new. When they have collected a few stickers, reward them with a prize, which should be agreed upon before you start so everyone knows what they are working towards.

Stay positive

Praise your child when they eat well, and keep cool when they don't. If you get angry or show your frustration you'll just escalate the problem. When they say they are done, simply take away the plate and don't comment. And don't offer anything else.

Keep it simple

Serve simple, healthy food, nothing too elaborate or strongly flavoured.

Children and junk food

Unfortunately, young or old, children have a real love of 'junk food' – sweets, snacks, take-aways, all the shop-bought grab-and-go food, which isn't nutritious and that we know they shouldn't eat but are so tempting to fill a hunger gap or a craving. And let's face it, we adults are pretty partial to these things, too!

When it comes to teaching your child about healthy eating, it is difficult to ban these foods completely, as they will inevitably encounter them at friends' houses, parties or as teenagers out with their friends. So the key here is to allow all foods, but make sure your kids understand that these should only be eaten occasionally, as a treat, and try to prevent them becoming the norm. If you simply ban a food you make it more desirable and it may become something they eat in secret!

To help everyone on this mission, try not to keep junk food around the house, and ensure there's a supply of healthier, quick and easy foods to snack on instead.

Feeling sad about losing the food you love? Why not feed the habit in a healthy way by making one night a week homemade take-away night? Make your own 'healthy junk food' – use good-quality lean mince to make burgers, prepare and top homemade pizza bases or use English muffins, or cook your own curries using a blend of spices and fresh ingredients. Chicken nuggets or fish fingers are so easy to make, too, coated with polenta, leftover breadcrumbs or cornflake crumbs from the bottom of the cereal box! You can make potato wedges or chips from potatoes or sweet potatoes to serve alongside.

For dessert, make your own yoghurt bombe (see page 194) rather than serving ice cream, or try the posh jelly jars (see page 197) instead of shop-bought jelly. For a treat, try making muffins, which will give you little lovely bites in appropriate portion sizes that will satisfy that sweet tooth.

Children vs vegetables – the great battle

When it comes to food fussiness it's often the healthy stuff that causes the most fights. While you may not expect children to be eating a vast range of these foods (although let's face it, that would be nice!), we all know it's important to find a few staple fruits or vegetables that they'll eat so you know they're getting all their essential nutrients from these and are on track to meet their 5 a day requirements. Here are a few tips on how to get them to eat the good stuff:

Make food fun

Really fussy eaters may come to dread mealtimes if you take the wrong approach, so make them something they'll look forward to instead. Little things can ease the fear and bring a smile to their face. Perhaps stand mini broccoli 'trees' in mashed potato snow, or make a snake from cucumber slices, or use red peppers to make smiley faces with carrot eyes or hair, or keep it really simple and serve up multi-coloured fruit kebabs.

Test the texture

For some children it's texture that's the issue rather than the taste. If they don't like cooked veg, try offering it to them raw instead – sticks of carrot, cucumber and pepper, baby sweetcorn and cherry tomatoes are easy and nutritious finger foods. They make great snacks, or a more filling lunch served with houmous, salsa or a cheesy dip. Cold raw veg sticks are lovely for hot, teething gums – but keep an eye on young children with finger food in case of choking.

Change it up

If your child particularly likes one type of food, work with this to see if you can stretch them to include other veg with it. If they love potatoes, perhaps serve a baked potato with a healthy topping such as tuna, or a cheese and broccoli sauce, or mash some potato and stir in some cooked cauliflower, carrots or peas.

Gloves are off

When in desperate measures, be sneaky. Grate carrot or courgette into stews or sauces, or dice veg into tiny cubes that won't be noticed. Hide white veg such as white parts of leeks, cauliflower or parsnip into white sauces and coloured vegetables into tomato sauces.

Get them involved!

Make mealtimes something that children can get involved with and take some pride in. Giving them a few simple jobs will feed their growing sense of independence – and help you out no end!

✔ Make mealtimes something that children can get involved with and take some pride in. Giving them a few simple jobs will feed their growing sense of independence – and help you out no end!

✔ Plan a menu for dinner together – let them draw pictures on it to show to the rest of the family, or practise writing if they're older.

✔ Go shopping together – let them touch and smell some of the foods and see what's on offer. Seeing all the colourful foods in different shapes, sizes and textures might get them interested in new ingredients.

✔ Let them cook with you – give them a job, let them add ingredients (sprinkle in some herbs or stir in the milk, for example), or just play with fruit or veg while you cook to allow them to feel the texture, or smell and nibble at it.

✔ Set the table – let older children lay out cutlery and plates. It gives them a job and also sets them up from an early age to help around the house.

Keep it in perspective

Ultimately, as long as your child is active and gaining weight, and they don't appear to be ill, they're probably getting enough to eat, even if it may not seem like it. However, if your child's fussy eating means that they're losing weight, or they seem lethargic and are weak or irritable, it's worth consulting your doctor.

So try not to worry too much; don't feel intimidated by other parents whose children eat everything, as long as your child is regularly eating one thing from the four major food groups – milk and dairy products, starchy foods, fruit and vegetables, protein – you don't need to worry. It doesn't even matter if it's the same food meal after meal, it's about the nutrients it offers – if your child isn't bored with the same food, there's no problem. Just keep introducing other foods alongside these and who knows, one day they might pick them up and try them!

The Wilsons

Meat free
and veggie

Meat-free Monday is a global initiative that was started to encourage people to give up meat one day a week, to benefit their health and the environment. If you're a carnivore, going without meat might not sound appealing, but read on and you might find the argument for it could convince you to make the effort just one day a week! Of course, you can pick whichever day suits you and, who knows, once you get into it you might make other days meat-free, too?

Going meat-free

Eating a plant-based or meat-free diet isn't a new concept, but in recent years it has become an increasingly popular way to eat. In fact, some sports stars have adopted a vegan diet as a way to improve their health, believing it has also helped them to perform at the top level. With this increased profile, the number of vegans in Britain has risen by 360 per cent over the past decade; there are now around half a million people in the UK eating this way.

Following a vegan or vegetarian diet is very much a personal choice, and there are many different reasons why people make this decision – some are concerned about animal welfare or the environment, some don't eat meat because of their religious beliefs or simply avoid it because they don't like the texture and flavour, while others choose to eat a largely plant-based diet for health reasons.

The Allisons

Vegan or vegetarian

Confused about what is what? Quite simply, a vegetarian diet eliminates meat, poultry and fish but usually includes eggs and dairy, while a vegan diet goes further and excludes all foods that derive from animals in any form – so not just meat but also dairy products, eggs and honey.

Health benefits of a plant-based diet

There are several health benefits to eating a plant-based diet, not to mention the benefit to your wallet.

By avoiding meat, vegetarians tend to consume less saturated fat and cholesterol and take in more vitamins C and E, fibre, folic acid, potassium and magnesium. If you eat mostly veggies and also cut back on refined sugars, salt, hydrogenated fats and saturated fats, you will lower your Body Mass Index (BMI), which should reduce your risk of heart disease and type 2 diabetes. As well as being good sources of essential vitamins and minerals, fruits and vegetables are an excellent source of dietary fibre, which helps maintain a healthy gut and prevents constipation, and can reduce the risk of bowel cancer. Especially good sources of fibre are cruciferous vegetables, such as broccoli, kale and cabbage; vegetables high in carotenoids, such as carrots and sweet potatoes; tomato products; and alliums, such as onions, garlic and leeks.

Most fruits and veg are low in fat and calories, too, which makes them a healthy snack choice – although be warned that dried fruits are higher in calories and sugar than fresh, so should be eaten in smaller quantities.

Avoiding meat does not mean following a diet based purely on fruits and vegetables. Most vegetarians also include cereals, pulses, nuts and seeds in their diet to ensure they get all the essential nutrients that their bodies require; whole grains and legumes, in particular, are important because they improve blood sugar control by slowing the rate of carbohydrate absorption and cutting the risk of diabetes.

Of course, any diet that restricts foods will inevitably restrict some nutrients. Non-meat eaters consume less protein than meat-eaters, but they can meet their recommended intake by eating whole grains and legumes, such as quinoa, spelt, lentils, peas, beans and soy-based products. Replacement iron that is usually sourced from meat can be found in non-meat products, such as beans, peas, lentils, green leafy vegetables, broccoli, nuts and oatmeal.

Depending on which plant-based foods you eat, if you adopt a vegetarian or vegan diet you will need to carefully analyse which essential nutrients you are including in your diet on a regular basis and consider taking supplements to plug any gaps. Of course, cooking from scratch is an ideal way to monitor your intake of all healthy – and unhealthy – ingredients, and by planning and preparing your own food you know exactly what you are putting into your body and what you are missing.

The Prestwiches

Eat your way to 5 a day

One of the huge benefits of a plant-based diet is that it's pretty easy to meet the guidelines of eating 5 a day. The advice from the World Health Organisation is that there are significant health benefits, including a lowered risk of heart disease, stroke and some cancers, to be had by eating a minimum of 400g of fruit and veg each day, which is broken down as at least five separate portions of 80g per day.

Eating veggie on a budget

Aside from the health benefits of cutting out meat from your diet, there are also considerable savings to be made. Meat and fish are often the most expensive food items in your supermarket trolley, and removing these or even just reducing the amount you buy will make a considerable impact on your shopping bills.

According to figures for 2014 from the Office for National Statistics, the average UK family spends £15.80 a week on meat and fish, with £4.20 and £3.50 being spent on fresh vegetables and fresh fruit respectively, so the maths is clear – reduce your meat intake and you should also reduce your expenditure.

However, if you feel that you can't do without meat entirely, try reducing the number of days on which you eat it, or use less of it in a recipe, bulking out the dish with more vegetables, pulses or beans. You will be getting an equally filling and delicious meal, with more fibre, at a much lower cost.

Here are a few tips to eating veggie on a budget:

Remember that fresh, frozen, tinned, dried and juices all count towards your 5 a day – fresh can be the most expensive, but all the other forms are just as nutritious and often cheaper, with frozen fruits and vegetables, in fact, having a higher nutrient content than fresh (see page 16). Food packaged this way also has a longer shelf-life than fresh, so there's less wastage if you don't eat it quickly.

Buy fruit and veg in season – buy from a local market for good prices, or buy in bulk or when on offer, and freeze what you don't need immediately (see page 37 for which are best for freezing).

Don't ignore the mark-downs – over-ripe fruit can be frozen when you get home or used in smoothies, ice cream, crumbles, fruit pies, etc. Vegetables that have seen better days and are going cheap can be used in soups, casseroles, stews, etc., or blanched and frozen immediately for another day.

Eat the rainbow

Your 5 a day should consist of as many different-coloured varieties of fruits and vegetables as possible. If you need a little inspiration to pick your selection, here are the benefits of the different pigments of fruit and veg:

Red

Tomatoes, red peppers, radishes, rhubarb, strawberries, raspberries, cherries.

Contain lycopene – an age-defying antioxidant, which may protect cells in the prevention of heart disease, protect skin from sun damage, and may also protect against certain cancers.

Orange

Oranges, nectarines, peaches, mangoes, satsumas, apricots, sweet potatoes, carrots, red lentils, baked beans.

Contain alpha- and beta-carotene – these get converted to vitamin A in the body, essential for vision, immune function and antioxidants that protect your skin from ultraviolet damage. Vitamin A also builds new cells and is good for bone health.

Yellow

Grapefruits, bananas, pineapples, sweetcorn, squash, yellow peppers, yellow lentils, chickpeas.

Contain beta-cryptoxanthin – a phytochemical that helps with vitamin and mineral exchange between cells. May also help to protect against rheumatoid arthritis and heart disease.

Green

Avocados, melons, gooseberries, apples, pears, courgettes, cucumbers, peas, spinach, lettuce/salad leaves, broccoli, cabbages, asparagus, kale, spring greens.

Contain lutein – a carotenoid that's good for skin hydration and elasticity, and helps to reduce the risk of cataracts and protects the eyes. Also contain isothiocyanates, which are anti-carcinogenic. Avocados and leafy greens are also rich in vitamin E, which can help prevent wrinkles and strengthens cell membranes.

Purple

Raisins, currants, sultanas, prunes, figs, damsons, plums, blueberries, blackcurrants, blackberries, grapes, aubergines, beetroot, kidney beans.

Contain anthocyanidin – this protects against pain and inflammation, may support healthy blood pressure and may also have anti-ageing properties by preventing the breakdown of collagen in the skin.

Batch cooking

Imagine coming home, opening the freezer and seeing a selection of meals ready and waiting for dinner that evening. And we're not talking shop-bought convenience meals – we're talking delicious home-cooked meals! Cooking in bulk is a brilliant way to make good use of your freezer and have you smiling at the end of a long day when your family is snapping at your heels demanding food.

Batch cooking couldn't be easier; if you've got the time, spend an afternoon cooking a few different meals to go into the fridge or freezer for the days or weeks ahead, or if time is short, just double or treble the quantities of a recipe you're cooking and freeze the extra portions.

If you do find the time, spending a couple of hours preparing a few meals really is time well spent; it means you've got a variety of dishes ready for you on busy days, which will make life so much easier. Still not convinced? Think of it this way, although you're increasing the amount of ingredients for one recipe, you are still only spending the same amount of time cooking and using the same amount of energy to cook it, but you're saving yourself a lot of effort on another day.

Tip

If you're soaking dried lentils or beans overnight for a recipe, prepare a larger quantity and cook them, then pop the extra in the fridge ready to be whipped up into a healthy side dish or salad the next day.

Why batch cook?

✔ It's a great way to use up any leftovers before you go shopping, or to make use of any bulk-buy offers so they don't go off before you get to them.

✔ It gives you the reassurance that there is something ready to cook in the freezer after a long day – either as a complete meal or the basis of one.

✔ Having your own food ready and waiting will keep you on track with healthy eating – if it's home-made you know what's in it, and if you're too tired to cook, it reduces the temptation to reach for a shop-bought ready meal.

✔ You can simply multiply the ingredients in the recipe, or add others to pad it out. For instance, you don't have to use double the amount of meat, instead bulk it out with extra vegetables and/or cooked pulses or beans – much cheaper than buying more meat.

Get organised!

Create the space – clear out your freezer ready to store your pre-prepared dinners. Have an 'eat from the freezer' day or two and organise a sort out to free up some freezer space.

Use re-usable containers to store your meals in – if they are microwavable you can get dinner on the table in no time by going straight from freezer to cook! Foil containers with lids are also a good bet for storage (but not for microwave cooking!).

Clearly label any food you store and include the date (see page 35).

Pin a list of what you have stored in the freezer somewhere in the kitchen (or on the freezer door) so you know exactly what's in there. Don't forget to cross off dishes when you use them!

Make sure whatever you're storing in the freezer is divided into portions so nothing gets wasted when you defrost it, as you can't refreeze it.

Brilliant batch recipes include...

- ✔ Curry
- ✔ Chilli
- ✔ Pasta sauces
- ✔ Lasagne
- ✔ Soup
- ✔ Stews
- ✔ Pizza bases
- ✔ Burgers
- ✔ Fishcakes

The Riellys

The Haynes

Leftovers

In these days of rising food prices, it may be alarming to discover that UK households throw away 7.3 million tonnes of food every year – which is around 19 per cent by weight of what we actually buy. According to WRAP – who work with governments, businesses and communities to find ways to prevent waste and encourage re-use and recycling – reducing this wastage could save the average family £60 a month, or over £700 a year, and deliver significant environmental benefits in reducing landfill.

Lots of us waste food because we don't plan our meals, or we buy more than we need. Sometimes we don't store food properly so it deteriorates quickly, or we don't understand what the use-by, best-before and display-until dates mean (see opposite). Some of us serve up too-large portions, or we just don't know what to do with leftovers.

The Brooks

Use-by date

This is about food safety and applies to highly perishable food. It is the recommended date by which you should use the product, and the only way this date can safely be extended is if the food is frozen. If not, store it as recommended on the packet and chuck it at the end of the day on the use-by date; after this date, the food shouldn't be eaten.

Best-before date

This relates to the quality not the safety of the food and is an indication of how long it will last. The food is at its best before the date given, and the flavour and texture will deteriorate after that, but it's not necessarily dangerous. Use your judgement about whether you want to eat the food past this date.

Display-until date

Some retailers mark food (especially fresh food and veg) with a 'display-until' date, but this is information for the shop staff only; consumers shouldn't confuse this with 'use-by' or 'best-before' dates.

So there's a huge opportunity for us to reduce our shopping bills simply by saving more food from going in the bin.

Love your leftovers

There are two sorts of leftovers: what's left from cooked meals and ingredients that are approaching the end of their life and haven't yet made it into a meal. So, before you bin it, think: can I still use it? You'd be surprised at what you can do to give foods one last chance.

If you're keeping leftovers from food you've already cooked, cool them quickly, off the heat, ideally within 1–2 hours, loosely covered, then transfer them to the fridge immediately once cold. If you have a large amount, spread the food out into a large, shallow dish so it cools quicker. Never leave food cooling at room temperature for hours or overnight.

You should only store your leftovers in the fridge for up to 2 days, no longer, so if you think you won't eat them within that time, try freezing them instead.

When you come to reheat, make sure the food is heated all the way through until piping hot. Don't reheat leftovers more than once. If you're reheating from frozen, ideally defrost the food thoroughly before cooking (in the fridge overnight is ideal), but if you're pressed for time you can defrost and reheat in the microwave (see page 38), but again, make sure it is heated right through with no hot or cold spots.

Reheating rice

Rice is the most thrown-away ingredient – according to WRAP, we chuck away 40,000 tonnes of it each year. Cooked rice can be reheated, but you do need to pay a bit more attention when doing this than you would with some other foods, as otherwise it can make you ill. If you want to save cooked rice for later, cool it as quickly as possible (ideally within 1 hour) and put it straight into the fridge, covered, then store it for no more than 24 hours. When you want to eat it, reheat it thoroughly in the microwave or in a pan, until piping hot all the way through.

The kings

What to do with leftovers!

Raw vegetables

Chop them up and use in stocks, soups and stews, or juice them for a healthy vitamin-packed drink. If you blanch them for a few minutes in boiling water and freeze them, they will stay really fresh and keep their colour, ready for cooking when needed. If you only have a few bits of veg but not enough to make a whole dish, pop them in a freezer bag to make stock at a later date. Cooked veg, particularly root vegetables, are great in frittatas as chunks, or mashed up to be used in fishcakes or fried.

Fruit

Over-ripe bananas are great for smoothies, banana bread, muffins or chopping into chunks for the freezer. Frozen chunks are great for making ice cream and smoothies. Apples, pears, plums, rhubarb and similar fruits can be stewed or poached and eaten as they are or in crumbles or pies, or frozen. Apples are also great as apple sauce. Very ripe berries can be puréed to make a delicious sauce or coulis, which can be eaten fresh or frozen for later use. Pretty much any fruit can be juiced, too.

Dairy

Parmesan rinds are great for adding a rich flavour to stocks and soups, just chuck them in and then scoop them out at the end. Old bits of hard or semi-hard cheese can be grated and frozen to add to sauces or gratins or just to sprinkle over food. If you're freezing whole chunks of cheese, defrost before using, but frozen grated cheese can be added to any dish that needs cooking as it will defrost and melt really quickly.

Milk

Milk freezes well, but make sure there is room at the top of the container as liquid expands on freezing. If you want to use the milk quickly, fill a washing-up bowl with hot water and submerge the milk container – it should be well-thawed after about 30 minutes; if time is not a worry, leave the container in the fridge and it should defrost within 24 hours.

Eggs

Whole eggs approaching the end of their life can be used to make omelettes or frittatas. Leftover egg yolks from a recipe can be used to make custard or mayonnaise, while whites can be used in meringues, mousses or to glaze bread. Both parts of an egg can also be frozen. Separate the eggs into freezable containers and pop in the freezer. Don't forget to label how many yolks or whites are in each container, so you know what you've got when a recipe calls for them.

Tip

To test an egg for freshness, lower it carefully into a bowl of cold water. If the egg sinks and lies on its side, it's fresh and good to cook; if it stands on one end, it needs eating fast; and if it floats – don't eat it!